EXECUTIVE
MEMORY
TECHNIQUES

EXECUTIVE MEMORY TECHNIQUES

Jon Keith

THE MEMORY TRAINER

A DELL TRADE PAPERBACK

A DELL TRADE PAPERBACK
Published by
Dell Publishing
a division of
Bantam Doubleday Dell Publishing Group, Inc.
666 Fifth Avenue
New York, New York 10103

ISBN: 0-440-50207-1

Printed in the United States of America
Published simultaneously in Canada

August 1989

10 9 8 7 6 5 4 3 2 1

MV

To the best memory experts
Lillian A. Keith
Florence A. Cestaro
Mortimer R. Samuels
Caroline and Edmund Antonacci
and to Patricia, Uncle Mike, Aunt Jane

———————

Special thanks to Maria Tesoriero,
a great friend,
and
MK, LS

Contents

NUMBERS

TAKING CARE OF BUSINESS

Introduction

A good memory is a necessary tool for today's business person. Most people in the business community today believe that you must be born with a good memory. However, the truth is that memory is a skill that anyone can develop with little effort. When an executive has a superior memory he will see a difference in his business life. He will feel more confident and his productivity will increase to new heights. If he is in a service business, his clients will be amazed that he will effortlessly remember their names and other details about them. The result will be new business. His friends will hold him in a higher regard, and his superiors will trust him with many more tasks. You see, the bottom line of Memory Training is confidence building. This translates into a superior business person.

This book will concern itself with methods of trained memory that will make your study time more meaningful. The methods come from history and have been proved by countless people. These people include the ancient Greek and Roman orators, who would speak for hours without notes. In the Middle Ages the monks used memory techniques to keep knowledge for the future. In the present business people use these devices to promote business and profits.

The techniques laid out in this book will provide an advantage for the person who puts some time and effort into learning them. When you put the time into learning the techniques outlined here, you will see a difference in your memory ability and confidence in a very short time. You will be able to recall as many names and faces as you like and will be respected and known as a genius. You will be able to remember long-digit numbers faster and retain them longer. Finally, you will have better reading comprehension for all types of reading material.

What you are about to learn is the art of trained memory. Yes, it is an art that can be learned and applied with little energy. This art is called Mnemonics. Mnemonics is the real word for memory training. What I have done with the art of Memory is to make it into a simple skill for the business person to use every day. My experience for the past seventeen years has been that of a teacher and motivator to the top corporations in America. In my research on the topic of memory I have found out that a relative demonstrated the art of Memory in the 1930s. This made me intensify my research to the point where I can teach the art of Memory Training in very simple terms. With this experience I will teach you the basics and demonstrate examples that will have you become an expert in very little time.

THE BASICS

SHORT- AND LONG-TERM MEMORY

Did you ever wonder why you can remember your first-grade teacher's name and not remember what you had for lunch? The answer is that you had more of an interest in the teacher's name than in the lunch. It is also because of Short- and Long-term Memory.

Short-term Memory can be imagined as a small holding pen for information. Long-term Memory can be seen as a permanent area of stored information. There is a track that information travels on from Short- to Long-term Memory. When you remember something it first goes to Short-term Memory. After a period of time, if you are lucky, it then goes to Long-term Memory, and thus it is stored for a long period of time.

This is the ideal scenario. In the real world you will forget information. Because you overstuff S-TM (Short-term Memory), information doesn't travel into Long-term Memory.

With Trained Memory more information travels the route to Long-term Memory. Therefore, it is easier to learn information with Trained Memory.

NATURAL MEMORY

This book will improve the efficiency of your memory! Right now your memory is capable of remembering many names and faces after meeting them once or of remembering any piece of information. You only need to train your memory. Anyone who can read and write can improve the efficiency of their memory.

You must apply yourself and learn the techniques in this book. Let us describe the difference between Natural Memory and memory-training devices.

Natural Memory is God-given memory without any memory devices. It is the memory that you have struggled with all your life. Mnemonics, on the other hand, is an organized method by which your Natural Memory can be prompted. Mnemonics is like a pin that someone might stick into you to wake you up, except that a pin is stuck into our Natural Memory to wake it up.

There is one very important point that many present-day memory experts ignore. Mnemonics (memory systems) must follow the same laws that your Natural Memory obeys. For example, if person A studies (crams for an exam) without using memory systems and person B crams using these systems, each will not use his memory to its fullest. Each cheats himself by cramming. Human memory is not a computer where information can be poured in and remembered. It is a natural machine that must obey Natural Memory laws.

THE LAWS OF MEMORY

The rules of memory (even when you apply memory-enhancing techniques):

DON'T cram.

DON'T study subjects too close together.

DON'T use alcohol when studying (it will impair your memory).

DON'T have a bad attitude (it will slow your learning the memory methods).

DON'T think mnemonics will make you into a human computer. You will have to make the effort to learn and apply the methods in this book.

DO follow the techniques exactly to develop a better business memory.

DO practice and learn the methods.

DO consult the book when you have questions.

DO use the 15–5 Method when you study (study for 15 minutes and then break for 5 minutes and continue in that mode). You will find an improvement in your study habits.

DO have fun with the techniques.

THE POPCORN RULES

The Popcorn Rules consist of a list I made up several years ago stating some Natural Memory methods you can use immediately. They are called the Popcorn Rules because you can remember the rules easily by the word "POPCORN" (and because I wanted to go to the movies). Each letter of the word "POPCORN" represents a rule. Here they are:

1) *Positive Attitude*   If you have an enthusiastic attitude toward remembering, your Natural Memory will eat up your material and you can improve your Natural Memory by 5 to 10 percent. If you wonder how to become positive, a simple way is to examine your goals.

If you need to remember a client list, think about the results from remembering the list—better client relations and success in business. You will find it is better to be positive in business.

2) *Observation*   Did you ever go to a big city or country town and see how the people walk? They walk in a straight line with their heads down, ignoring what is going on around them. To have a better Natural Memory, you must take notice of your surroundings. When you do this your Natural Memory improves automatically.

3) **Picture It**   With this idea you come closer to the heart of the memory methods presented in this book. It is called the Mind's Eye. Is there a third eye? In a matter of speaking, yes. For example, do not think of the Empire State Building. What is happening? Yes, you are thinking in picture form of a piece of the building, the whole structure or some kind of image.

Your Mind's Eye is like a video picturing device in your mind that can help your Natural Memory and is used in conjunction with memory methods. So the next time you want to remember something, picture it. Actually see that telephone number or errand in that third eye.

4) **Concentration**   If you have paid close attention to the three previous hints, you have been concentrating. It is difficult to tell someone to concentrate on one single task, but concentration is connected with memory. You will find that your concentration level will be higher when you use the Popcorn rules and mnemonics.

5) **Organization**   If you organize the facts that you have to remember, you will retain them longer. There was a study some years ago in which a group of people (Group A) had sixteen household items to remember in a given set of time. The list was presented as follows:

spoon, screwdriver, pan, gloves, stove, plate, blanket, flashlight, pillow, hammer, sheet, garbage pail, pliers, lamp, drill, bed.

Another group of people (Group B) had the same items to remember, but there was a difference. Look at the items that Group B had to remember:

spoon, pan, gloves, stove, plate, garbage pail, screwdriver, flashlight, hammer, pliers, drill, blanket, pillow, lamp, bed, sheet.

You see that Group B saw the items organized into related groups. The result was that Group B remembered the items faster and retained the list longer. If you want that type of improvement, get organized!

6) **Review It** The way to properly review is to use your vocal cords, and actually say out loud the material you want to remember. Studies have proven that using the vocal cords stimulates Natural Memory. But never review this way while walking down the street!

7) **Natural Association** When faced with a memory obstacle that reminds you of something in your past, use that image. This will lock it in your memory because it is from your personal experience. For example, say you have to remember the number 747-1939. First, examine the number. The number 747 reminds most people of a plane so use that image. Actually see that plane in your Mind's Eye. Next, look at 1939. That number may remind people of the New York World's Fair or their old address. It does not make any difference as long as you see that picture. With this simple rule you can see an improvement in your memory immediately.

These rules are the basis of all Natural Memory methods. I give them to you as a warm-up to the rest of the book!

Now you must be thinking, "How does the author remember three hundred people's names and faces after meeting them only once or remember an entire magazine in one hour?" Very well! Actually the answer is with the art of Trained Memory. Right now I want you to be prepared to learn a skill that will help you for the rest of your business life!

TRAINED MEMORY

Trained Memory is a method by which a person develops a system of reminders so that Natural Memory can reproduce the material. As stated earlier, these techniques are as old as man himself. It is not a new invention, but people like me are always trying to make the techniques easier to learn.

The steps for a person to train his or her memory are Association, Replacement, and Application.

ASSOCIATION

"How do you associate?" When told to link two objects together, most people will look for similar characteristics. In a mnemonic sense, this is incorrect. The mind can remember ridiculous images in great detail. You will take advantage of this fact in a very novel way. To help you learn the first step in our memory system, I will give you the classic rules of Association. They are:

1) exaggeration
2) switching
3) motion

These rules come from history and they work great! For example, let us associate two items: cigarette and door.

When most individuals are asked to do this task, they will picture cigarette and door together. This is wrong, simply because it is not ridiculous enough. A better picture would be a door smoking a cigarette, which is an example of **Exaggeration.**

Yes, I know, what you are thinking is that this is very silly and impossible. By **Exaggeration** your mind will remember the two items because the association is impossible, silly, and stupid. That image will remain in your mind because impossible images usually stick in one's memory.

How about **Switching**? Take the two items and interchange them. You can see a giant cigarette as a door or a pack of doors (miniature size) instead of cigarettes. It's like a cartoon. Don't worry if you can't get the images immediately. It takes practice. Let's go to the next example of the rule of Association.

An example of **Motion** would be seeing many cigarettes coming at you when opening a door.

There are a few points to remember:

1) When associating use the rule that you are most comfortable with.
2) Don't worry about retaining that ridiculous association because in time it will fade and you will remember the items.

You must practice what you just learned by associating the following pairs of items. Remember, you are in the warm-up stage of your memory training. You have to use concrete, familiar items in the beginning to master the art of Association. Association is the glue that you are to use to remember a name and a face, a long-digit number, or reading material. Practicing with familiar items is almost like the runner training for that big race. He doesn't run the big race unless he trains on familiar ground and masters his running technique.

Here are the items:

Clock–Car

Let me help you with the first couple of pairs. Here are my suggestions. You could picture yourself entering a giant clock-car, or see a car on your wall in the form of a clock, or finally see many clocks coming out of your car.

Pen–Oven

You could see yourself cooking a large pen in your oven. Another suggestion would be writing with a big oven and having a hard time.

Radio–Boat

You could see a big beautiful radio moored to your dock or see a giant boat in your living room playing music.

These are my suggestions for a ridiculous association between the items. Now you will have a try at association. Associate the following items:

Door–Cigarette	Film–Lamp
TV–Chair	Camera–Person
Picture–Car	Hose–Book
Computer–Hammer	Plaque–Nail
Dish–Cigar	Ball–Grass

Did you have fun? Don't feel discouraged if you had a problem associating the pairs. Most people who begin this skill have a little problem with this exercise.

The solution is to practice association and to stick with the skill and not to give up. Remember, you must master the method of a ridiculous association. This is the real key to the Memory System.

THE INFO-CHAIN

The Info-Chain is the basic part of any memory system. It is the device that allows information to enter your memory correctly and stay in Long-term Memory. But to develop it you must learn to expand associated pairs of items to form chains of items. This will permit you to practice the art of Association.

Suppose you were given a list of items such as the following: cigarette, door, clock, desk, car, and TV set.

I know what you are thinking: "I can associate only two items, so how will I remember six items?" However, with the idea of an Info-Chain, you can connect the entire list of items in pairs of two. For example, take the first two items, cigarette and door. Let's think of a ridiculous association between them. One association that demonstrates the rule of exaggeration is to think of the cigarette, that is, a large cigarette opening the door and walking through it! To demonstrate the idea of movement, see, as you open the door, many cigarettes coming in the door. An association to demonstrate Switching is to see a giant cigarette instead of the door. Right now, as you are reading this, I would like you to try to associate along with the examples.

Using Association (pick your favorite—Exaggeration, Motion, or Switching), you are going to connect the items in a long Info-Chain! Now back to the list. You have associated two items—cigarette and door—by seeing them in your Mind's Eye. Now the third item is a clock. What is the last item in the first association? That's right, it was door. Now you are going to take door and clock, and associate.

Then to help you associate for the last time, let's take a couple of examples between door and clock. You could see the hands of the clock as giant doors or see a giant clock open a door and walk through it, etc.

The most important idea is to choose only one association and to see it in your Mind's Eye. What happens to cigarette and door? Well, nothing. While you are associating the other items you don't have to worry about the beginning of the Info-Chain because at the end of this lesson I will show you how to remember the first item.

Remember, I want to train you to trust your memory. If you have the tendency to go back and think of the other portions of the Info-Chain, *DON'T!*

The last item on our list that we mentioned was clock. You are now going to connect clock and a new item—desk. You could see, as an example of an association, a giant clock sitting at a desk working.

Now associate the next item. The next item in our Info-Chain is car. The last item was desk. Let us connect the two items. Picture a desk driving a car. Or you could see someone driving a desk. It does not make a difference what picture you use because your Natural Memory will tell you the correct order of the list. Our next item is TV set. To complete the Info-Chain, you could see a TV set instead of your car and actually see yourself driving it. Or you could see a car instead of TV set in your living room. Since this was the last item, let us review.

If you repeat the list out loud once or twice, you will notice that the ridiculous associations you choose begin to fade, and you know the items without the aid of the pictures. This is how Association really works. When you create an association this way, the Association eventually will fade, and the information will become locked in your permanent memory (Long-term Memory). The purpose of this exercise is to master Association. You will be amazed at how you can repeat the items backward and forward. Some people worry about forgetting the first item and not remembering the list. If you are really worried, you can associate the first item to the door of your house or apartment.

It is this type of association to something that is in your memory already, that will lock the first item in your memory.

This exercise should be practiced (using different items) until you have mastered the art of Association (in fact, the Info-Chain can be used with a little imagination to remember things to do, etc.). To get you started use the Info-Chaining idea to associate the following lists (you should try to associate one list at a time at your own pace):

Stove	Car
Rose	Computer
Bat (Baseball)	Boots
Sailboat	Wallet
Light Bulb	Pan
Telephone	Picture
Camera	Record
Window	Piano
Pen	TV
Book	Dog
	Fence
	Store
	Dress
	Ring
	Pizza

That was an interesting exercise to help you to master the art of Association. To help you further, I will give you my associations to Info-Chain the previous lists. Developing your own associations will make them stick in your memory. Remember, our purpose is to make associations like a chain, that is, two items at a time.

Stove—Rose   See a giant rose growing out of the stove

Rose—Bat   See a baseball player using a giant rose

Bat—Sailboat   Imagine a giant bat as a boat

Sailboat—Light Bulb   Actually see a sailboat screwed into a light socket

Light Bulb—Telephone   Use a light bulb as a phone

Telephone—Camera   Use a telephone as a camera

Camera—Window   See many cameras as windows in your house

Window—Pen   See yourself using a window instead of a pen

Pen—Book   You are reading a giant pen

Here are my associations for list number two (remember, you are Info-Chaining):

Car—Computer   See yourself driving your computer

Computer—Boots   You are putting on your computer instead of your boots

Boots—Wallet   You have a boot in your pocket as a wallet

Wallet—Pan   See yourself using your wallet as a pan in the kitchen

Pan—Picture   You have a giant pan on the wall instead of a picture

Picture—Record   Your picture is on the record player

Record—Piano   See a giant record as your piano

Piano—TV   See a TV set playing a piano

TV—Dog   You are walking the TV set

Dog—Fence   See your dog as the fence around the house

Fence—Store   See a giant fence around your favorite store

Store—Dress   Your favorite store actually in a dress

Dress—Ring   See a small dress around your finger

Ring—Pizza   Instead of cheese, there are rings on your pizza

Don't be discouraged if you have a problem making the associations. You only need practice!

THE 1-2-5 REVIEW TECHNIQUE

When using the methods of memory in this book, you will need a proper way to review the material. I have created the 1-2-5 Review Method. When you have the material memorized, using your associations, you will follow the following review schedule:

Day **1** you review only once
Day **2** you review only once
Finally, Day **5** you review once (you skip the third and fourth days)

When using the 1-2-5 Review you will find by the fifth day you are able to recall the material without the use of the associations. This is because they have done their work in capturing the material and sending it to Long-term Memory.

The temptation is to go over the material many times. This is called rote memory. I call rote memory the unorganized monster. It is a waste of time and will not effectively permit the material to be memorized. But when using the methods of memory in this book and the 1-2-5 Review Technique, the material you are memorizing will go to Long-term Memory.

THE POP EFFECT

When you use Association with the other techniques in this book, you will experience a very interesting effect I call the Pop Effect. It is having the information you associated popping into your Mind's Eye.

This can be a real help when you are in a business meeting and someone you met last month approaches you with a smile. At this point you realize that you do not remember the person's name. This is when the Pop Effect takes control. At the last possible moment the name jumps into your mind and that person is amazed at your memory.

It is my opinion that the Pop Effect is the subconscious mind taking control for a second, telling your Natural Memory where to find the material. Enjoy the effect, it's there for your business benefit!

You will now start to learn the next basic step to a great memory, which is the art of Replacement.

REPLACEMENT

Using this simple technique, a person takes an abstract piece of information and forms a picture representing the information. This helps you retain the information because your visual memory is much better than your verbal memory.

The best way in which to demonstrate this is to learn a very unique and effective way of remembering a word and its meaning.

WORD POWER

You can use Association and Replacement to build your Word Power. To demonstrate Replacement take the word "pasquinade," meaning a lampoon, and say the word *aloud.* Then try to picture an image to represent the word in your Mind's Eye. The image has to be concrete and picturable. You could picture a masquerade or the phrase "pass the grenade" for the word. Both replacements are great but you need to picture only one replacement to remember the word.

For attaching the meaning to the word, you use Association. You could see everyone at a masquerade holding a harpoon or see a group of people passing a grenade with a harpoon in it.

With Association and Replacement you could increase your Word Power rapidly. Here is another example, the word "cadge," meaning to get by begging. "Cadge" can be replaced by the image of a cage. Connecting the word with the meaning, the association would be a giant cage in the street begging for money.

To review, here are the steps to a better vocabulary:

A) Say the word aloud.

B) Replace the word with a picture in your Mind's Eye.

C) Replace the meaning with a picture.

D) Associate the two pictures.

Remember, this process takes only a matter of seconds. You will develop speed with practice!

Word-Power Exercise*

Using the technique you just learned, associate the following words and their meanings:

*With the help of The American Heritage Dictionary of the English Language (New College Edition).

1) dole—a gift of money given as charity

2) cairn—a mound of stones piled up as a landmark

3) besom—a twig broom

4) akimbo—the hands on the hips with the elbows turned outward

5) hew—to cut with repeated blows

Answers to the Word-Power Exercise

1) dole—a gift of money given as charity
You can see a giant pole (telephone) giving out money as charity.

2) cairn—a mound of stones piled up as a landmark
See thousands of convicts (cons) piling up stones as a monument.

3) besom—a twig broom
See a bee and its son sweeping the floor with a twig broom.

4) akimbo—the hands on the hips with the elbows turned outward
Imagine a smart bow (a keen bow) as a person with his elbows turned outward.

5) hew—to cut with repeated blows
See a rainbow (hue) with hands cutting a log with repeated blows.

You are ready to learn a method that will help you conquer the number-one memory problem in corporate America, which is the remembering of a name with a face.

NAMES AND FACES

HOW TO CONNECT A NAME WITH A FACE

The main memory problem in the business world today is remembering a name with a face.

It is important to remember a name and a face because this is a powerful tool that anyone can use to excel in their careers. For instance, you are going to a sales meeting and at this meeting you are to meet fifteen top business executives.

What do you think they will say about you when you talk to them after the meeting and remember their names? I can tell you it will be very positive. Here is another example:

You go on a sales call and meet the entire staff at your client's company. When you phone several days later, with the technique of remembering names and faces, you will have full command of the situation on the phone. You can break down barriers just by remembering the receptionist's name. You can request the person you need to speak to by name and department. This skill can also be used as an opening to new business.

Still another example is that you are in a business convention and meet and remember several people. This may not sound like an earth-shattering experience, but when you are in a business environment you must have full command of the situation. You will find when you approach these people again during the convention, they will probably be amazed that you remembered their names, and that can open the door for any type of business pursuit. What I am saying is simple: Know a **name** and **success** will follow! And now to the process of remembering a name and a face.

THE TECHNIQUE

Most people remember the face of a person but not the name. The reason is that the face *is* a visual picture in the Mind's

Eye and the name does **not** present any visual impression. You must turn the name into a picture. Once you have that picture representing the name, it is associated to a feature on the face. You must master picturing a person's name first to make it easier to learn the rest of the technique.

Using your imagination, you can picture any name. This is accomplished by using Replacement. For example, my last name is Keith. What does Keith sound like—teeth, key, thief?

They all will fit the definition because you can use your imagination to picture the name in your Mind's Eye. You need to just picture some of the name to complete the process of Replacement. Let's take another example: the last name Samuels.

Samuels is not a hard name to visualize. Every name can be pictured if you only use your imagination. You could use the picture "some mules" in your Mind's Eye to replace the name. Remember, the idea of Replacement is to set a reminder in action so that your visual memory will be prompted into giving the correct information. The replacement will fade and you will have the information in Long-term Memory.

You must master the technique of picturing a name. The following is a list of names that I want you to, as fast as you can, transform into a picture. This exercise is very important. If you master this technique, you will be able to master the total method for names and faces with ease.

Now let us practice this method of converting a name into a picture. Convert the following last names into a picture in your Mind's Eye.

Hooper	_____	Otis	_____
Irving	_____	Bauer	_____
Kaufman	_____	Campbell	_____
Jeffries	_____	Brady	_____
Oppenheim	_____	Gibbons	_____
Neil	_____	Forrester	_____

Harper	_____	Hally	_____
Cestaro	_____	Lennz	_____
Levine	_____	Zachary	_____
Joyce	_____	Williams	_____
Lilly	_____		

Answers

Hooper—hoop
Irving—nerve
Kaufman—cough man
Jeffries—jump freeze
Oppenheim—hop and rhyme
Neil—nail
Otis—Oh! this
Bauer—bow (and arrow)
Campbell—camp bell
Brady—brandy
Gibbons—ribbons

Forrester—forest
Harper—harp
Cestaro—just stare
Levine—the vine
Joyce—juice
Lilly—lily pad
Hally—hall
Lennz—lens
Zachary—sack
Williams—a will

After this exercise I would advise that every time you hear a name, you try to convert the name into a picture. In this book there are first- and last-name pictures for you to look over as a practice for your new business tool. This will get your memory into shape and make the technique easier to apply.

Now you are ready to start the process of learning the method of remembering a name and face.

Hear the Name

When people are introduced they usually never hear the name of the other person. They walk away wondering, "What was that person's name?"

Therefore, the first rule of all memory systems for remembering names and faces is to hear the name of the other person. That's right, hear the name. If people just did this, they would increase their remembering of names by approximately 10 percent. If an individual mumbles his name, don't hesitate to ask it again! If he does not want to give his name again, WALK AWAY.

Just kidding. I have met and been introduced to thousands in my seminars, and not one person has refused to give me his name again.

Feature Scanning

For the next step you must pick a feature or features on a person's face. My method of selecting a feature is called Feature Scanning.

This method involves you looking with your eyes in the following pattern:

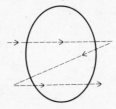

What you are seeing is the path of your eyes when you are introduced to a person. Don't worry about the other person noticing you while you are Feature Scanning. The movement of your eyes will not be noticed.

When you apply the method of remembering a name and a face, you will find that every face is different. It doesn't matter if the people you are remembering are twins. There are differences. The way an individual trains themselves to pick a feature is to practice. The way we practice in this book is with photographs. Are you ready to test your ability to select a feature?

Feature-Scanning Exercise

Please list the features you would pick if you were to meet the following people:

There is an infinite possibility of features to select from the photographs. For example, eyes, nose, lips, hair, eyebrows, eyelids, neck, hair color, glasses, lips, chin, shape of face, etc. Remember, these are photographs. Imagine real faces!

How does one practice this method of picking a feature? It is an easy task. You just follow my steps to remember a name and a face and you will have all the practice you will ever need.

If you stopped here, you would improve your memory for names and faces about 15 percent. The reason is that you are paying more attention to the person's name and face and forcing yourself to remember. Unfortunately, this way of remembering has limits and takes more energy than the technique you are about to learn.

So far you can make a name into a picture and isolate a feature on a person's face. It is almost like the Info-Chain in that you have two items to unite, that is, a picture for a name and a feature on a face. The glue to unite the two items is Association.

THE COMPLETE SYSTEM

You are ready to put what you have learned to work. To review, when you meet a person you:

A) Hear the name
B) Select a feature (using Feature Scanning)
C) Make the name into a picture (using Replacement) you can see in the Mind's Eye.

Most people would think the previous steps would take too much time when meeting people in a business situation. In reality these steps, with practice, will become one process and will take a second or two. In order to get to that level we need practice. You will now meet several people and I will walk you through the entire technique of remembering a name and a face. The first person is Ms. Schider:

First, you select a feature. The feature that stands out in my mind is her eyes. I don't want to select the feature for you because I will not be in the next business situation with you! You must select it on your own. If you selected another feature, use it. The next step is taking her name, Schider, and making a picture from it. Her name sounds like spider and that would be a good picture. Using the Mind's Eye, you want to connect the feature and the picture you made from her name. You could imagine a giant spider in her eyes or see the spider on any feature that you selected.

What you just did with the simple association was to focus on the name and face in a unique manner to burn it into your memory. It is the same process as Info-Chaining, two items in a long list. The only difference is that you associated a feature on a person's face and a person's name (in picture form). Some people may feel a little uneasy with this technique. The cure for these people is to go out and practice. It will be worth the effort when you see the results of being able to recall people's names and faces in a business environment.

The key activity for you is to practice this technique so that you are comfortable. The next person to meet is Mr. Schuloff:

This is Mr. Schuloff. The first step is to pick a feature. I selected his mustache. I know that he can shave it off, but Natural Memory will still tell me his name. In my opinion, the unconscious brain examines the surrounding features as well as the main feature to ensure the association will remind you of the name even if he shaves off the feature. To get this backup system to work, you must consciously select one outstanding feature.

Now the name, Schuloff. Using Replacement, what can you picture for the name? Skull-off would work. You have the feature, and the name is in picture form. You now can associate to unite the two pictures, that is, the feature and the name. You could see his skull flying off his mustache or you can see a skull as his mustache and maybe see it coming off.

These two are great associations, but you must see only one in your Mind's Eye. Try not to constantly think of the association, just do it and then go on to the next name and face.

You need to practice. Now I want you to meet some of my friends (don't worry if you can't picture the names or associate, I will have my associations for the names and faces of my friends to help you develop your association skill later in the book). With this exercise I want you to apply the complete system for remembering names and faces. Let's meet:

Ms. Keogh

Mr. Mulroundy

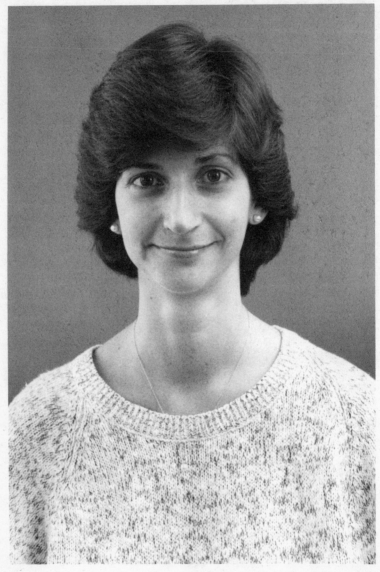

Mrs. Bulcheesy

Mr. Brimes

Mr. Cestaro

Ms. Goldberg

I know what you are thinking: "This process is hard!" And to that statement I say, "Good." You should not worry about speed, but know the technique. I will now give my associations for the names and faces of our friends. By going over my associations it will help push your imagination in forming associations using this technique.

Ms. Keogh   The first feature that I see is her glasses. You can use the glasses if you pick them. Now to the name. The name Keogh reminds me of keyhole. A good association would be seeing two large keyholes that look like glasses. But I must remind you, the associations are seen in your Mind's Eye only.

Mr. Mulroundy   The feature I saw was his round face. So I replaced his name with mud around his face. I saw a lot of mud around his face.

Mrs. Bulcheesy   She has beautiful eyes so I picked them as the feature I would use in the association. I saw a bull with cheese in its mouth in her eyes. Now you must realize that you are seeing that image in your Mind's Eye only.

Mr. Brimes   Immediately I thought of salty water (brine) and associated that mixture all over his high cheeks.

Mr. Cestaro   His nose stood out, so I associated a giant chestnut with his nose. Using the Switching idea of Association, I saw his nose as a large chestnut and I am staring at it (this idea of staring is to get the pronunciation of the last part of the name).

Ms. Goldberg   I picked her forehead as the feature and saw a large iceberg of gold on it.

If you had some trouble with the associations, don't give up! Remember, this is a new skill you have to continue to develop. Let us see how to remember first names with last names.

First Names

You have to make a choice in business. Are you going to meet people by their first or last names? Usually people introduce themselves by their last names. I would advise you to associate their last names first, then attach the first names.

First names are remembered by the same method. The only difference is that, with the last name already in place, it is easier to make the association. It is almost like putting together a jigsaw puzzle. Once you have the main pieces in place, that is, the last name, the rest is easy.

Let's take a full example. You are introduced to yours truly, **Jon Keith.** The first thing you notice is my mustache. Then you make my last name into a picture, for example, key. The association is simple—a giant key in my mustache. Congratulations, you have my name. Now you go for my first name, Jon. How about a picture of a vanity from a bathroom for Jon. Remember, you connect the first name to the last name just as you connected the items in an Info-Chain. Just connect the vanity to key (maybe hanging the vanity on the key).

There you have it, a complete example. Remember, the associations you make to attach a name and a face are temporary and will *fade*. Association is the process that helps the name and face travel the track from Short-term Memory to Long-term Memory. When the association fades, the name and face will remain in Long-term Memory.

To review: To remember a first name when a last name is already associated, you just connect the first name to the last name as an Info-Chain.

Now let us meet our friends again, but this time with their first names:

Ms. Cathy Keogh   Mr. George Brimes

Mr. Frank Mulroundy   Mr. Dennis Cestaro

Mrs. Elaine Bulcheesy   Ms. Eileen Goldberg

If you go over the faces (without cheating), you will find that you will remember their names, but you need to develop the skill even further.

Here are some suggestions for the first name replacements for our friends:

Ms. Cathy Keogh—To picture Cathy try a large cat (a tiger).

Mr. Frank Mulroundy—To picture Frank try frankfurter (maybe attached to a feature?).

Mrs. Elaine Bulcheesy—To picture Elaine try "the lane" (a road coming out of a feature?)

Mr. George Brimes—George translates to gorge (I will leave you alone to associate this one!).

Mr. Dennis Cestaro—Dennis can be pictured with a giant dent in his face.

Ms. Eileen Goldberg—I am seeing myself leaning on her face.

Name-Picturing Exercise

In this skill for remembering a name and a face, the hardest part is to picture a name. In this exercise you will practice picturing first names as a warm-up to the skill. This will make your applying the technique easier in the real business world. In the following exercises make a picture for the following names that you can visualize in your Mind's Eye:

Bob   ——————————

Fawn   ——————————

Joan   ——————————

Fran   ——————————

John   _____

Barbara   _____

Gary   _____

Tony   _____

Sheila   _____

Florence   _____

Doug   _____

Frank   _____

Cliff   _____

Nester   _____

Bo   _____

Guy   _____

Silva   _____

Joy   _____

Steve   _____

Denise   _____

Jay   _____

Pat   _____

Eve   _____

Elaine _____

Brandy _____

Wendy _____

Serena _____

Jo _____

Mike _____

Charles _____

Rob _____

Chris _____

Robert _____

Zak _____

Penny _____

Keith _____

Mitchell _____

Jerry _____

Harry _____

Jane _____

Art _____

Sally _____

Lucy   _____

Monte   _____

Jean   _____

Cathy   _____

Ruth   _____

Ron   _____

Hilda   _____

Lil   _____

Calvin   _____

Daisy   _____

Ed   _____

Balwin   _____

Mattie   _____

Jonah   _____

Answers to Name-Picturing Exercise

Bob—bobcat

Fawn—dawn

Joan—loan

Fran—fan

John—a john

Barbara—bar

Gary—carry

Tony—tone up

Sheila—shield

Florence—flora

Doug—dig

Frank—frankfurter

Cliff—cliff

Nester—nest

Bo—bow

Guy—guide

Silva—silver

Joy—toy

Steve—stiff

Denise—dent

Jay—jaybird

Pat—a pat (on the face)

Eve—Xmas Eve

Elaine—the lane

Brandy—brandy

Wendy—windy

Serena—serene

Jo—show

Mike—a microphone

Charles—char

Rob—rob

Chris—crystal

Robert—robot

Zak—zap

Penny—penny

Keith—key

Mitchell—my shell

Jerry—cherry

Harry—hairy

Jane—chain

Art—artwork

Sally—saddle

Lucy—loose

Monte—mount

Jean—jeans

Cathy—cat

Ruth—root

Ron—run

Hilda—hill

Lil—lily pad

Calvin—cow man

Daisy—daisy

Ed—head

Balwin—ball win

Mattie—mat

Jonah—loan her

The most difficult part of the method is to form a picture from a name. To give you an edge over this obstacle, I am about to give a sample of my pictures for first and last names.

The pictures I am giving you are the images that I use every day when I am introduced to people. Some require that you use your imagination to see the pictures. Don't memorize the images, but just look them over, using the 15–5-minute study approach (mentioned in the beginning of the book). Also, make sure you are not tired when going over the Name Pictures list. In my research I have found that people who looked at the Name Pictures found it easier to picture and associate a name with a face. This can also be used as a reference for your new technique, but don't carry this book with you when meeting people. It will get in the way!

FEMALE FIRST-NAME PICTURES

Abby—a bee

Agnes—a nest

Aida—first aid

Alice—a glass

Amy—aim (rifle)

Barbara—bar

Bea—bee

Belle—bell

Beth—bath

Brooke—stream

Camille—a meal

Candace—can of lace

Candy—candy

Carmel—caramel

Caroline—carry a line

Dale—ale

Edith—eat it

Eileen—I lean

Elizabeth—lizard

Ellen—L in

Etta—ebb

Fanny—fan

Farrah—pharaoh

Fern—fern

Flo—flora

Fran—fan

Gail—gale

Georgia—gorge

Gerry—merry

Gloria—glow

Golda—gold

Haley—comet

Hannah—banner

Harmony—music

Helen—hell

Holly—holly

Ida—eyed her

Ina—inn

Irene—my ring

Iris—iris

Ivory—ivory

Jackie—jockey

Jade—jade

Jane—chain

Janet—a net

Jewel—jewel

Kara—carat

Karen—carat in

Kate—cake

Kitty—cat

Kyle—tile

Lane—lame

Laura—law

Lena—len

Lily—lily

Linda—lint

Mabel—marble

Maggie—mag wheels

Mamie—mane

Mary—marry

Meg—peg

Nan—bland

Nell—kneel

Nikki—nick

Noel—noel

Norma—normal

Ophelia—feed her

Olga—old

Oliver—olive

Oneida—I need her

Opal—opal (gem)

Pat—pack

Paula—pull

Peg—peg

Phyllis—fill this

Pia—pizza

Quin—gin

Que—cue ball

Randi—ran

Raven—raven

Rebecca—beg

Robin—robin

Ruby—red ruby

Sally—saddle

Sandy—sand

Sheila—shield

Sherry—sherry

Stella—cellar

Taffy—taffy

Tamera—hear her

Tammy—tan

Terry—terry

Tina—team

Uri—curry

Ursula—curse

Valerie—valley

Venus—Venus

Wanda—wander

Whitney—whip

Willa—will

Winona—granola

Xena—zinc

Yetta—net her

Zen—lens

Now let us continue by listing Male First-Name Pictures.

MALE FIRST-NAME PICTURES

Abram—a ham

Adam—a dam

Adler—add it

Andrew—draw

Arthur—art

Barnett—bar in a net

Barry—barrel

Ben—bend

Bill—dollar bill

Boyd—bird

Cal—cow

Calvin—cow in

Carver—carver (wood)

Charles—charred

Cole—cold

Dallas—doll

Dan—dam

Devin—devil in

Doug—dig

Duke—a duke

Ed—head

Egan—gun

Elliott—idiot

Elton—a ton

Erhard—a heart

Falkner—a fork

Ferris—ferry

Filmore—fill more

Flint—flint

Forest—forest

Galvin—gavel

Gene—jeans

George—gorge

Giovanni—gee a van

Grady—a grade

Hall—hall

Hamilton—handle a ton

Hamlet—omelet

Harry—hare

Herman—he-man

Ingram—in a telegram

Irving—nerve

Irwin—I win

Isidore—there's the door

Ivan—van

Jack—car jack

Jake—rake

James—chains

Jay—the letter J

Joe—hose

Kane—cane

Keith—key

Kennedy—half-dollar

Kevin—cavern

Knox—ox

Lance—lance

Lars—tar

Leo—keyhole

Lester—a nest

Lincoln—penny

Madison—mad

Marc—mark

Matt—mat

Mike—microphone

Mortimer—more tea

Nat—gnat

Nick—nick

Noel—Xmas

Norman—normal

Olin—lint

Oliver—olive

Orion—a lion

Orlando—land

Otto—otter

Paco—pack

Palmer—palm

Pat—pat (hand)

Paul—pull

Porter—port

Quincy—wince

Rainer—rain

Ralph—growl

Ray—ray

Rich—rich

Sam—sandwich

Sandy—sand

Saul—salt

Sawyer—saw

Sherwood—sharp wood

Stan—stand

Tanner—tan

Terry—terry (cloth)

Tim—timber

Tom—tomcat

Truman—true man

Udell—you doll

Upton—upon a ton

Van—van

Vance—lance

Victor—victory

Vincent—a cent

Vito—veto

Waite—wait (sign)

Waldo—wall oh!

Ward—ward

Washington—President

William—yams

York—fork

Zane—insane

I will now give you the pictures I use for last names. Remember, it is okay to create your own picture for a name, but once you have a picture for a name, don't change it.

By now you will have an easier time picturing the names, but continue to review the list. It will give you the practice you need to start the skill of remembering names and faces!

LAST-NAME PICTURES

Alberts—all burp

Alder—older

Allcott—all the cots

Anderson—hand and son

Applegate—apple on a gate

Beastly—beast

Beers—beer

Bosworth—boss worth

Brent—rent

Butterworth—butter worth

Calle—cow

Cestaro—just stare

Collins—collar in

Cosgrove—cars drove

Cox—lox

Deerland—deer land

Doolittle—draw a little

Drake—rake

Drew—draw

Drummond—Drum's mound

Ellis—a wrist

Elmont—the mount

Engle—angle

Evert—invert

Eyles—the nest

Figoli—figs all over

Franks—frankfurters

French—French

Folly—fold

Flower—flower

Gassley—graze

Gates—gates

Glossie—glossy picture

Goodman—good man

Grant—President Grant

Henches—hens

Hinkley—ink

Hite—height

Hogs—hogs

Horton—a heavy hawk (a ton)

Isadore—there's a door

Ises—ice wrist

Inforiti—in a fort

Ingle—angle

Innes—in a nest

Jacobs—hiccups

Jaeger—jagged

Jaworsky—jaw on a ski

Johnson—a John

Jones—owns

Karp—harp

Kay—a giant K

Keith—key

King—king (crown)

Kitt—kitten

Lacey—lace

Laid—lai

Lister—listen (an ear)

Little—little

Looms—a loom

Malone—my loan

Marino—marine

Miller—miller (the profession)

Moore—moor

Morris—more rice

Nally—rally

Nelson—melting sun

Nesbitt—nest bite

Nickles—nickles

Nun—nun

Oakes—oak tree

O'Brien—it's bright

O'Dell—dill pickle

O'Hara—the hare

Oliver—olive

Paley—pale

Perkins—put in

Perry—period

Pine—pine (wood)

Plum—plum

Poll—a poll

Quail—quail

Quan—swan

Queen—a queen

Quick—quick

Quinn—inn

Quirk—work

Rafferty—raft trees

Reagan—ray gun

Reice—rice

Richardson—rich son

Ross—gloss

Saker—sick

Salzman—salt man

Samuels—some mules

Schaeffer—safer

Scott—cot

Tanner—a tan

Taylor—tailor

Thomas—the mass

Thornton—thorn that's a ton

Tyler—tile

Udall—a doll

Udea—your tea

Understead—under the spread

Van—van

Vance—lance

Victor—lick

Vito—veto

Washington—President

Watts—watts (electric bulb)

Welsh—a well

West—the old west

Xaras—Czar

Xavier—blazer

Xenkas—zinc

Xerxes—jerky

Ximenes—small men

Yang—yank

Yard—yard

Yellin—yell

Young—young

Yuke—nuke

Zack—sack

Zagar—sick car

Zarro—narrow

Zigler—zigzag

Zue—zoo

That was a long list of the last names that will give you a start in this skill. As you know, you are faced in business with names from around the world. These names can be tough to picture. But you would be a better business person if you could remember every name, including your overseas clients. Imagine your superiors when they find out you are the only one in the company who can remember those names.

It is in that spirit that I am giving you Name Pictures for my favorite tough names. Review them the same way as the other Name Pictures. Here they are:

Wong—dong

Kamura—come here now

Nakagama—nab a gown

Misiura—missed tour

Tiso—tease

Jampatom—jam at home

Jrhosaboy—a horse to avoid

Kunsaitis—cone at this

Muhlenbruch—lend me a brush

Cauterucci—halter that's itchy

Georgacopou—a gorge and a cop

Haimowitz—ham on white

Pfluger—a fluke

Amechazurra—a mess of swords

Borkenhagan—broken handgun

Ekmekjian—a mess in an oven

Malinowsky—mallet on a ski

Harshavardhana—hogs on a hammer

Intrabartola—in a bar and fall over

Reussille—red silk

Novobilsky—nobel on a ski

Avalishvilli—have a wish on a hill

Gasiorowski—gas on a ski

Roleke—roll key

Sheremeta—share some metal

Nakamura—naked mural

Ishihara—is it hail yet?

Tschurko—this cork must go

Ongsiako—one sack to go

Tinari—tin art

Kapighian—a cap behind

Laurenzano—law in sand oh!

Kirchdoerffer—crush a door sir

Lysandrov—the sand is off

Divinagracia—devil in glass

Isganitis—is it gone?

Nisivoccia—miss the boat sir?

Coppolecchia—cop on a pole

Baltadonis—bolts and doughnuts

Fikkema—fit a camera

Ehrenfreund—errand free

Musorrafiti—you must fit

Campaniolo—a camp pan hold it

Dellapietro—deal a pie and throw it

Ottombrino—I'll bring you

Onouchak—on a jack

Fiumefreddo—fumes from a radio

Paluchowski—pour the chow on the ski

Santomauero—phantom aura

Susnoski—don't sue the ski

What a list! Don't get discouraged, because after a period of time, using the technique, you will be able to make a picture from any name in a matter of seconds.

Picturing a Complete-Name Practice

I think you need some more practice with complete names. Here are some practice names with features. They won't have pictures with the names. All you have to do is to associate the replacements for the names to the feature mentioned.

1) Pat Ruddy—her feature is very high cheekbones.

2) Florence Antonacci—her feature is large eyes.

3) Mort Samuels—his feature is an odd-shaped nose.

4) Michael Copa—his feature is a high forehead.

5) John Smith—his feature is a long face.

1) Pat Ruddy—cheeks; you could see very **ruddy** cheeks then **pat** the cheeks with your hand.

2) Florence Antonacci—eyes; you could see **an ant in a notch** in her eyes and that ant is holding a **floral** piece.

3) Mort Samuels—sharp nose; you could see **some mules** on his nose and that mule has **warts.**

4) Michael Copa—high forehead; see a **cop** on his forehead and the cop is holding a **microphone.**

5) John Smith—long face; you could see a **blacksmith** on his face and the blacksmith is hammering a **vanity** (for the name John).

These are the pictures I would use to remember the names of these people. I give them to you in order to teach the technique. I would hope that it encourages you to create your own pictures for names, but it is all right to use my pictures. If you create your own picture for a name, stay with the picture; don't change the image every time you meet a person with that name.

Eventually a name will automatically become a picture in

your Mind's Eye. To get to this point takes practice but it will come in very little time. The bottom line is that you use the system!

What you need to do now is practice. From now on, when you read the newspaper, every time you see a name and face in the paper I want you to use the technique. This will have a very good effect on the method since it is the easiest way to practice. Don't be afraid to use the technique immediately.

NAME AND FACE +

In corporate America there is more to learn than a name and a face. Usually people are associated with a company or a product, and sales depend upon people remembering these connections. This can be accomplished by Info-Chaining the piece of information to the Name Picture, which is connected to a feature on that person's face. At this point you can connect a name and a face, so we are attaching information only to the Name Picture. I know when you see a feature on a person's face you will remember the name and the name will lead you to the rest of the information. Consider the following examples:

1) Mike Fisher works for a computer company in their disk development department.

2) Deb Ragens works for a telephone company in their sales department.

3) Steve Framer works for a video company in their business office.

4) Pat Bloom works for a bank in their safe-deposit department.

5) Nick Wells works in an electronic pager service company as a consultant.

To remember this information with a name and a face, you will Info-Chain the information to the picture of the name. Look at Mr. Fisher.

There are three pieces of information to remember. The first thing is the name Fisher. Let's picture the name. The picture I would use is that of a fish. Fish is the first on our Info-Chain; the second is computer. This can be visualized by picturing a computer keyboard.

Now let's associate. Using Switching, you're typing on a fish instead of a computer or you could see a fish working on a computer. This is the first connection or association. It doesn't matter what association it is as long as you see the picture and use it. What you do now is Info-Chain the next piece of information (like your first Info-Chain list in the beginning of the book).

The next piece of information is the disk department. You connect this with computer keyboard, which is the last piece of information on our Info-Chain. You could see a giant disk working on a computer keyboard.

Maybe you could see a giant computer keyboard destroying your entire disk library (an image that you would never forget).

It really doesn't make a difference what image you see as long as you associate correctly according to one of the rules (Exaggeration, Switching, or Motion). Now, with the Info-Chain in your head, when someone asks about Mr. Fisher, you have the answer.

Remember, the connections fade as it travels to Long-term Memory and the entire process of Info-Chaining will become faster as you apply it.

If you want to remember Mr. Fisher's first name, you simply connect it to the Info-Chain. A picture for Mike could be a microphone. You could see a fish singing into a microphone, and thus you have complete Info-Chain on Mr. Fisher. Consider the next example. Remember, try to do the examples as quickly as possible. This will help you develop the technique and speed.

Look at Deb Ragens. The name Ragens can be pictured as a ray gun. The telephone company can be pictured as a phone and the sales department can be pictured as a sale sign. Now you create an Info-Chain! The first connection is ray gun to phone. You could see yourself picking up a ray gun instead of a phone.

Another image that comes to mind is seeing yourself shooting the telephone with a ray gun. This will connect the name with the company. The last piece of information is sales department, which we represent as a sale sign. You could picture a giant pile of phones (millions of phones) with a sale sign on top of the pile of phones. Remember, you are forming an Info-Chain.

To remember the first name attach the picture for the name Deb to the picture for Ragens. You could connect debutante to ray gun and see a debutante shooting a ray gun. That would complete the Info-Chain.

Steve Framer is the next example. For his name you could picture a picture frame. The next thing to connect on our Info-Chain is the video company. Visualize a large frame taking a picture with a video camera. Business office is the next thing to connect on our Info-Chain. See a video camera working in a business office. That is it! You have the information in a form that will cause you to remember everything about Mr. Framer.

Next is Pat Bloom—bank—safe-deposit department. Picture Ms. Bloom as a broomstick and connect it to bank. Maybe see a giant broom sticking out of a bank vault? Now connect bank to safe-deposit department. See a giant safe-deposit box as a teller in the bank. You could see yourself walking into a two-story safe-deposit box instead of a bank. That connects bank to safe-deposit department. Now you have your Info-Chain. Next time you see Ms. Bloom you will ask her about safe-deposit rates.

And finally Mr. Wells—electronic pager service—consultant. The Info-Chain:

1) You are carrying a small wishing well on your belt instead of a pager.

2) Actually see a large pager as a consultant working at a desk.

You see, the more you practice, the easier it becomes to connect the pieces of information with a name. It will reach a point when **ANY** Info-Chain will be connected in a matter of seconds.

VOICES

At this point you can remember many pieces of information using the Info-Chain method. You are going to learn a technique to remember voices and information on the telephone. As you know, this technique can be very important in the business community. If your company were involved in a million-dollar deal and the second party called your group and you forgot their name on the telephone, would that party do business with your company again? I think you get the point. Remembering a voice is just as important as remembering a name and a face.

Another example is a company where every receptionist would know the technique of remembering a name and a voice over the telephone. This company would have a powerful edge over the competition.

Remembering voices is easy. You will call upon the Replacement System to help. With this method any voice can be pictured. Consider Mr. Gardner, who has a smooth voice. Well, you can picture Gardner (a gardener) and you can picture a smooth voice. Just think of something that is smooth—maybe maple syrup. Great! Now you can make an association. You can see a gardener covered with maple syrup (he would be great for the bees).

The next time you hear that smooth voice on the phone, you will know it is Mr. Gardner. It will make Mr. Gardner feel great that you remember him. If he worked for a computer company, and you wanted to remember that fact, you would connect that fact to the last thing on your Info-Chain. See that gardener covered with maple syrup typing on a computer and you have a great association (and you will remember the company too). This will make a reputation for you and advance your career whether you are in a small company or a big corporation.

Another example is Mr. Novello, who has an Italian accent and is from a stationery store.

He is very important because your company has placed a large order with him and you must remember his voice and name. The first step is to picture the name Mr. Novello. It sounds like novel low. You can picture a large novel (book) on the floor (low) and you are reading it from a chair (sounds really crazy but it will work). The Italian accent can be pictured as anything that reminds you of Italy. My picture (and weakness) is a plate of pasta. You can connect it by seeing yourself reading a low novel and spilling some pasta all over the book. It does not matter if you connect the picture of the voice first or the name first. Your Natural Memory will tell you the difference. Just as you did in the Name and Face + section, you can connect an additional piece of information by Info-Chaining it to the last thing you associated. To remember stationery store you can see yourself writing with spaghetti on stationery. The next time Mr. Novello is on the telephone line, you won't have to stumble with your memory.

To get you started I have compiled a list of voice-pictures for you. Here they are:

Voice–Pictures

Smooth—maple syrup	Hoarse—horse
High—balloon	Authoritative—police
Squeaky—door	Weak—little person
Rough—sandpaper	Slow—dunce cap
Gravel—gravel	Loud—loudspeaker
French accent—Eiffel Tower	English accent—Big Ben
Huffy—the wind	Monotone—a flat board
Fluctuating—a wave	Cracking—popcorn

These are just a few voice pictures I use every day. At this time I know that you are thinking: "If I use these pictures all the time, won't I get confused?" The answer is NO! When you associate correctly, the name should "jump" into your head when you hear the voice. This is a form of the Pop Effect you read about in the beginning of the book. It seems that Natural

Memory has the ability to sort out the qualities of voice when attached to a picture. This sorting ability helps you to distinguish the voice and information.

You must realize that with imagination Info-Chaining can be a very useful business tool. Don't limit yourself in creating new ways to use it.

An Alternate Technique for Names and Faces

For those who still think the skill for remembering names and faces is too hard to master or want a quick way of improving their memory for names and faces, I am about to give a Natural Memory method. When you meet a person and hear his/her name, try to spell the name in your Mind's Eye. Even if you do not know how to spell the name, try! You will see that this method, although not as effective as Association, will help you to remember more names. You will also notice that you will remember their appearance as well. My preference for names and faces is using the method of attaching a name and a face by Association.

Some Helpful Hints

A) Don't try to become a memory expert overnight. With the excitement of learning the Trained Memory Technique for names and faces, some people try to learn everything in one night. Remember one of the natural laws in the beginning of this book—Don't Cram!

B) When meeting people take your time. As you progress with the Trained Memory Technique for names and faces, you will find that you can remember names and faces faster. As you use the technique your mind will store Name Pictures automatically. Eventually there will be no work in creating the images. The key is to use the Trained Memory Technique for names and faces as soon as possible. Don't wait! Under test conditions I remembered forty names and faces on a TV talk show in about two minutes (using the same Trained Memory Technique for names and faces), so do not get discouraged.

C) Be prepared to have people be jealous of your new technique for remembering names and faces. This can cause problems in an office setting, but if you are confident, nothing can stand in your way.

D) Customize the technique to your needs. Experiment with the technique. Make it easy for your mind to develop the method. If you only pick a feature on a person's face, you will increase your memory for names and faces by 15 percent. Imagine if you use the method 100 percent. The sky is the limit.

Summary for Names and Faces

Remembering a name and face uses Association and Replacement. Association is the glue that connects the name, which is a picture, and the face. This is done using the Mind's Eye and the rules of Association (making a ridiculous association between the name and face, etc.). To begin you pick a feature using Feature Scanning. This involves moving the eyes along the face in a "Z" fashion in order to pick a feature or features. When you have a feature you use Replacement to picture the name.

This is accomplished by hearing the name and using your imagination to form a Name Picture in the Mind's Eye. The next step is to make an association between the Name Picture and the feature that was selected. For example: Keith can be pictured as a key. I will now give you several examples of attaching the Name Picture to the feature using the rules of Association.

Using the Switching rule of Association, you would see in your Mind's Eye keys instead of my eyes.

Using the Exaggeration rule of Association, you would see a million keys in my eyes.

Using the Motion rule of Association, you would see two keys coming out of my eyes.

Remembering first names is the same method (Tom = tomcat, Mike = microphone, etc.). If you wanted to remember both first and last names, you would Info-Chain one to the other. Finally, when you remember a name and a face with this method, you are able to put that name and face into Long-term Memory with ease.

To remember a name and a face you:

A) Hear

B) Scan

C) Replace

D) Associate

NUMBERS

CORPORATE NUMBERS

In business life you are constantly faced with numbers to remember. These range from appointments, phone numbers, extension numbers, pass numbers to parking-lot numbers (you don't want to lose your car). You can improve your number memory with an easy technique using Association and Replacement.

I will walk you through the basics and provide exercises so that you will master the methods in a short time. If you apply the technique for remembering numbers in your work schedule, you will have a very powerful memory for numbers and greater confidence in yourself.

THE SOUND SYSTEM

A few centuries ago several people invented a system to convert a number into a picture.

The problem with remembering numbers is that they are just figures in your mind. If you can make a number into a picture, then you can use the techniques you know to remember the number.

First, you must learn a sound system that converts a number into a picture. This sound system has been pushed and abused in many memory books in the past few years. If you have an open mind and you are willing to learn a method for remembering numbers that will help you every day of your business life, then you will have no trouble with the technique.

Don't worry about learning the sounds because I have streamlined the memory cues that allow you to quickly learn them. Now let us look at the sounds:

1 = T, D

2 = N

3 = M

4 = R

5 = L

6 = J (Ch, Sh, soft G)

7 = K (hard G, C)

8 = F, V

9 = P, B

0 = Z, S (soft C)

This may seem complicated, but you will learn the sounds in a few minutes if you continue to read and trust your Natural Memory! With that assurance let's continue with learning the method.

You are interested only in the SOUNDS of the letters. All other sounds are discarded. You need to be patient and go step-by-step learning this technique for remembering numbers.

To learn the sounds so that they become second nature, use the memory cues. These are used in the beginning to get familiar with the sounds. As you use the sounds the memory cues will fade and you will know the sounds without their help. As I stated before, I have improved the memory cues to make the sounds easier to learn. Here they are:

1 = T, D   The one has one downstroke and so do the **T** and the **D**.

2 = N   The two has two downstrokes and so does the **N**.

3 = M   Think of three downstrokes and you will also think of **M**.

4 = R   If you make the 4 into a capital R 4 you will make the connection.

5 = L   Make the capital L into a 5 L and you will make the connection.

6 = J   Think of the **J** as a hook grabbing the 6 by the loop (also the sounds Sh, Ch, soft G).

7 = K Think of seven whipped-cream cakes (cakes sound like **K**) in a row (also the sounds hard G, C).

8 = F, V Think of eight—**FIVE** dollar bills in your hands.

9 = P, B Think of the 9 as a smoking pipe standing and the P as its opposite (the B has the same sound as the P so you will remember it too).

0 = Z Think of the expression "Oh! I **Z**" (instead of "Oh! I see") representing 0 and Z; the Z will remind you of the sounds for S and soft C.

There they are! These are the sounds you must master and I am going to help you remember numbers. There are some other things you must know before you begin to practice.

First, the sound for the number 6 is J and also sounds Sh, Ch, and soft G. Second, the sound for the number 7 is K and also hard G and C. Lastly the sound for 0 is Z, S, and a soft C. These additional sounds should not confuse you because they are the same basic sound as the original and with practice will naturally fall into place. Remember, the reason you have the memory cues for the sounds is just to get you to know the sounds paired with the numbers.

As you practice you will come to realize that you will not need the visual association to recall the sounds.

NUMBERS PRACTICE

You must know the sound system to master the total process of remembering numbers. The only way to make sure you know the sounds is to use a practice exercise. The following will help you to incorporate the sounds into your Long-term Memory so that you will have no difficulty in applying the total technique for remembering numbers.

In the following exercise convert the words into numbers using the sound system:

jelly	bulldozer
television	Chinese
battery	semigloss
gold	sailboat
table	Manhattan

What I want you to do is to use your new sound system and convert the words into numbers. Don't be tempted to look at the answers.

The way that you practice the sounds is to say the word slowly. JELLY. If you do that, you will have the number 65. Did I fool you? Did you have 655? Most people would put the double number there because they see two of the letter L in the word "jelly." You must remember that you are concentrating on the *sounds only,* not the number of letters in a word.

Hopefully, when you were doing the exercise you were not looking back to the page with the sounds. But if you did look back, it would just reinforce the sounds in your Mind's Eye. To develop speed in this process of remembering numbers, you must try to use the memory cues to learn the sounds. Here are the answers:

television = 15862   bulldozer = 95104

battery = 914   Chinese = 620

gold = 751   semi-gloss = 03–750

table = 195   sailboat = 0591

Manhattan = 3212

As you see, the process of conversion is very simple. Again, the only thing to watch for is the double letters (that are in our sound system) in words. These letters convert to a single number. Another example of this is battery. This word breaks down into 914, not 9114.

Memory students invent ways to learn to convert numbers into words. Consider putting sounds above the number. For example:

K, R, T or D, Z or S
7410

This number could be converted to the word "cards."

This is done only in the beginning to give some students confidence in their ability to work with the sounds. Other students play games with the sounds like writing a sentence with numbers and letting their friends try to decode it. This is just to speed their learning the sound system. I mention this to give you encouragement in learning to use the sound system. The bottom line of all this student play is to make it easy to put the total Trained Memory Technique for remembering numbers to work!

The Total Technique for Remembering Numbers

Once you are familiar with the sounds, you can build the rest of the technique. Look at the following number:

104

Let your mind relax and then convert the number into a picture. Take the sounds you know and verbalize them. The 1 can be a T or a D sound; the 0 can be a Z or an S sound, and finally the 4 is an R sound. You can say that the word "DICER" would fit the number.

Let us look at another number:

344

The first sound is an M sound. The next is R, followed by another R. Just say the sounds and you would have the word "MIRROR."

Let us try this number:

$$432$$

Using the system, we get the word "ROMAN." Up to now you have translated sets of three-digit numbers into pictures. If you had the same sets of numbers in a row as a long number, you could remember the total number by Info-Chaining. Here is how it would work:

$$104344432$$

$$104—344—432$$
dicer—mirror—roman

Now you can associate. Remember, you are Info-Chaining, that is, taking the first and second image and associating. Then you take the second and third image and associate, and then you continue in this fashion until the Info-Chain is completed. This type of Association in pairs will allow you to remember the number forwards and backwards. The number will be like an Info-Chain in your Mind's Eye. That is, like one image with associations that will fade and you will remember the number in the end. Now to the Info-Chain:

You could see a PERSON DICING (a DICER) many mirrors, then see a giant MIRROR as a ROMAN soldier. By associating this Info-Chain, you would have remembered a nine-digit number (something your local IQ test evaluator would love). Remember, the images will fade away and your Long-term Memory will be left with the number. Let us try another number:

$$275734481127$$

The first step is to translate the number into a series of pictures, and then connect the pictures by Association. This is the order of applying the technique I would suggest for all my students.

The number 275 translates into NICKEL. The next three digits are 734. This can turn into CAMERA. Now the association: You could see a giant **nickel** taking a picture with a **camera**. Now to the next three digits. The number 481 can translate to the word "RIVET." See a giant **rivet** in your camera lens (a picture that you won't forget). Finally, 127 can be pictured as TANK. See a giant **rivet** as a **tank.** If you followed along with the association, you could close your eyes and see the Info-Chain.

The main problem you will encounter in this process is converting the number into the images. This will become easier when you start applying the technique in your business world. I suggest you handle three numbers at a time and translate them into pictures. This will make it easy to apply the technique in the beginning, but if you see a five-digit number that can translate into one picture, use it. It is up to you to find those pictures in the numbers.

A successful business person will find this method one of the most powerful tools at his or her command. The reason is simple: They have to remember many numbers. For example: phone numbers, extensions, computer passwords, style numbers, zip codes, addresses, prices, bond yields, etc. All you need is practice. Here is an exercise that will help you (don't remember all the numbers in one sitting; save some for a later study time):

Long-Number Exercise

Using the process you just learned, make up an Info-Chain (picturing and associating) for the following numbers:

1) 794835217098

2) 5749366254827264

3) 400746390539267438201

4) 84736210798653724037674 9282

Long-Number Exercise Answers

1) 794835217098

keeper-family-new tack-zip off

Info-Chain Association You are a zookeeper caging your family; in your family there is a new member, a giant new tack (at the dinner table); see a giant new tack zipping off your bulletin board.

2) 5749366254827264

locker-buy match-channel-raven-quench-ray (for 4)

Info-Chain Association A gym locker is using a bought match to light a cigar; a bought match jumps out of a book of matches to change the channel of your TV set; out of a giant channel you see a thousand ravens (don't let the picture of a channel with a thousand ravens allow you to think that you are going to add a 0 to 482; the Pop Effect and Natural Memory will remind you of the correct number 482, raven); see a giant raven quenching his thirst with a drink (the Q in quench sounds like a K, 7); and for the last digit see a large ray of light quenching your thirst.

3) 4007463905392674438201

roses-crash-maps-lamp-no jack-remove-nest

Info-Chain Association See roses crashing into your car; see two maps on the highway involved in a crash; you can see many maps as a large lamp in your house; your lamp works with no electric jack; you see yourself removing all the electric jacks in your house (no jack); then see yourself removing a giant nest in your yard.

4) 84736210798653724403767749282

fork-machine-desk-buy fish-lamb wig-nurse-my cash-crop-uneven

Info-Chain Association You are eating a machine with a fork; see a machine working at a desk; at the market you see a large desk in line to buy fish; you have a lamb wig on to buy fish; see a lamb wig on a nurse; see a nurse take my cash; my cash is a crop in a large field; see acres of giant crops, uneven in shape.

Remember, when Info-Chaining in this manner for numbers, the Pop Effect will tell you the exact order of the images and thus the number.

Now to some applications in the business world:

PHONE NUMBERS

The first application is basic to survival in the business world—the remembering of phone numbers. If you can remember a large number (you just did that), then you can remember a seven-digit phone number. The only difference is that you must associate a name to the number.

The solution is easy: Just replace the name with a picture. You can then connect the pictures.

Consider the following fictitious phone number:

Mr. Webster 348-3619

You can picture Webster as a spider's web. For the number 348 you could use the idea of a MuRPHy bed, and for 3619 MatCHeD uP would satisfy the rules. Putting it all together, you could see the following Info-Chain: **web** to **Murphy bed** (a bed that retracts from the wall) to **matched up.**

Using the Info-Chaining Technique, you see a giant web sleeping in a Murphy bed and then see a person that matched up a thousand Murphy beds. Once you associate the number, it will stay in your Short-term Memory until it eventually becomes part of your Long-term Memory.

To speed up this process a review is required. You will use the 1-2-5 Review Technique. That is, you review once the first day, review once the second day, and on the fifth day when you review you will find that the associations begin to fade out of your mind. At this point the number is entering your Long-term Memory.

Some people will worry about remembering to review the second and fifth day. Your Natural Memory will prompt you to review the material. It is almost like an automatic red flag that will remind you to use the 1-2-5 Review Technique.

Here are a few fictitious phone numbers in order for you to practice the method of remembering numbers. The following are some examples:

Ms. Burns 427-5210

Mr. Hamton 702-6902

Mr. Forter 750-1640

Ms. Michaels 950-4910

Remember, you are to picture the numbers and form Info-Chains. The names are just another block of information to connect on the Info-Chain.

Here are the ways I would picture the names and numbers:

Name Pictures	*Number Replacement*	
A) **burn**	<u>rink</u>	**wal<u>nut</u>s**
Ms. Burns	4 27	52 10

Now you must make an Info-Chain with the pictures. You could see yourself burning a rink, then see yourself eating small rinks instead of walnuts. Remember, use your imagination. You must realize that the pictures are temporary, and in a short time you will remember Ms. Burns's telephone number without the images. Here are the other phone numbers:

B) **ham—ton**	<u>casino</u>	**<u>ship</u>s <u>in</u>**
Mr. Hamton	7 0 2	6 90 2

Info-Chain Association See a heavy ham (that weighs a ton) playing in a casino; see a casino on many ships in a harbor.

C) **fort**   <u>coals</u>   <u>teachers</u>

   Mr. Forter   7 50   1 6 40

Info-Chain Association Imagine a fort with large coals as soldiers; see a school with teachers using coals instead of chalk.

D) **microphone**   <u>bells</u>   <u>rabbits</u>

   Ms. Michaels   9 50   4 9 10

Info-Chain Association You are using a microphone with bells on it; you see many rabbits in a field, ringing bells.

Phone-Number Exercise

Practice using the technique for remembering numbers on the following fictitious names and phone numbers:

1) Mr. Bright 471-6734

2) Ms. Dishe 945-7543

3) Mr. Lea 854-7410

4) Ms. Zuelo 943-5140

Phone-Number Exercise Answers

1) Mr. Bright 471-6734

   bright light-rocket-show camera

Info-Chain Association   You are shining a bright light on a rocket and it lifts off; see a rocket as a giant camera and you are showing it to your friends.

   2) Ms. Dishe 945-7543

      dish-pearl-cow alarm

Info-Chain Association   You are wearing a large dish instead of a pearl; you are putting a pearl on a cow and an alarm goes off.

   3) Mr. Lea 854-7410

      lea (a meadow)-flower-crates

Info-Chain Association   You are walking in a lea with giant flowers (8 feet tall); then you see a flower moving crates.

   4) Ms. Zuelo 943-5140

      zoo-broom-ladders

Info-Chain Association   See a zookeeper as a broom; then watch a large broom climb up and down several ladders.

   Here are several other examples that you may encounter in the business environment:

BONDS

   If you look in the paper at the bond market, you could apply the technique to remember bond yields, etc. For example, let us look at this fictitious bond report:

Bonds	Cur Yld	Vol	High	Low	Close
KeY 9.75	35	127	101	95	92

All the information can be Info-Chained to be easily remembered. Let's translate the information into pictures: KeY = key; 9.75 = pic_kle (to represent the decimal point, see dots on the pickle and Natural Memory will then place it in the right position); 35 = mill; 127 = donkey; 101 = toast; 95 = bull; 92 = bin. Now the easy part—you associate the pictures. If you think of the bond, it only translates into a list of pictures that you can Info-Chain together (key, pickle, mill, donkey, toast, bull, bin).

Since you are a memory expert, you will Info-Chain very quickly. You could see a giant key in a pickle jar, then see a paper mill producing pickles.

You could see a giant mill on a donkey, then butter a donkey instead of toast.

Finally, picture a piece of toast as a bull in a bullfight, then that bull in a small bin. That's all you have to do! Remember, you are doing the Info-Chaining in your mind and that is quicker than reading it in this book.

You can use this technique to remember the entire bond section of the newspaper or just one bond quote. In any case, you will have the business edge.

If you find yourself in a situation with a fraction like ⅞, all you do is make the division bar into a picture. Using your imagination, it could look like an ax, a pencil, a pen, a crack in a wall, etc. When you decide on the picture just use the Info-Chain method. To remember ⅞ you could see a **cuff** with an ax in the middle of it (pretty gruesome). Or see a **cave** with a giant crack in the wall to represent the division bar. When you Info-Chain this way you will remember the entire piece of information.

FUTURES

Let us look at a fictitious example from the futures market:

Lumber

	Open	High	Settle
July	169.00	170.00	171.02

To remember the futures quote you use the Info-Chain method. You take care of the month as if it were a word to be pictured, using Replacement. July can be pictured as the Fourth of July, that is, maybe a firecracker. Then the rest is simple—just Info-Chain the pictures. You can start with firecracker, tou<u>ch</u> up for 169, <u>t</u>i<u>cks</u> for 170, and finally <u>t</u>i<u>cket sun</u> for 171.02.

The Info-Chain could be the following: a firecracker is touching up your house (with paint); see a giant tick touching up a wall (painting); finally a large tick giving out a baseball ticket to your son, who has dots all over his face (to represent the decimal point). If you don't have a son, use your imagination. When recalling the number you will notice that Natural Memory, because of the dots all over your son's face in your association, will tell you where to put the decimal point. Please make sure your connections obey the rules of Association (Exaggeration, Switching, and Motion).

REMEMBERING ON THE TRADING FLOOR

If you are in a stock exchange environment, that is, on the trading floor, you will have to remember a stock, to buy or sell that stock, and the quantity while traveling from one counter to another. This is accomplished by our old standard, the Info-Chain. To speed up the process I have created a picture representing buying or selling of stock. The picture I would use to sell would be a "For Sale" sign.

The picture I would use to represent buying is a credit card. Here is a fictitious example:

You must sell 4 shares of Jon Keith stock.

Info-Chain Association See a "For Sale" sign with many hares around it (you represent 4 by the picture ha<u>r</u>e) and see that rabbit with many keys (Keith).

With this technique you can remember many orders on the trading floor.

AT THE COMPUTER TERMINAL

With the advent of the computer in the office, your memory will have to hold vital operating information. Again, this can be solved with the Info-Chain. Here are some fictitious examples:

You are to remember the 1) File # 125 for entering the system;
2) Key # 3.8 for editing.

You use the Info-Chain to connect the number and function.

1) File # 125 for entering the computer system.

Info-Chain Association   125 converts to tunnel and you see a tunnel at a desk turning on and entering the computer system.

2) Key # 3.8 for editing.

Info-Chain Association   3.8 converts to movie (a giant dot on the screen to represent the decimal point) and you are editing a computer system in the movie theater.

It is up to your imagination to create Info-Chains for remembering in the world of computers.

ZIP CODES

With the advent of the new zip codes I must mention this memory obstacle. All you have to do is apply the Info-Chaining concept. Here is a fictitious zip code:

63940-5410
This can translate into chambers—lords.

Info-Chain Association   See many chambers (rooms) and medieval lords in them. Then take this Info-Chain and connect it to the person who has the address.

A PICTURE FOR EVERY LETTER

In the business world you will encounter letters in conjunction with numbers. You can remember letters by picturing them as you did with numbers. You start by creating a method in which you can picture the alphabet in your Mind's Eye. The alphabet can't be associated unless you use this method.

The following is a classic method from history (which I updated) to picture the alphabet. It uses pictures that sound like the letters themselves. This permits you to learn the pictures quickly. The system is not perfect, and you may have to use your imagination to visualize the letters. I would suggest that you review the method once or twice, then read on (you will be surprised how many Alphabet Pictures you will know). Here are the Alphabet Pictures:

A) ape

B) bee

C) sea

D) dean

E) eel

F) fork

G) G-man (federal agent type)

H) H-bomb (a mushroom)

I) eye

J) jaybird (use your imagination)

K) cake (with whipped cream)

L) elevated railroad

M) ember (in a fire)

N) inn

O) Oh! (picture the symbol !)

P) pea

Q) cue stick (pool)

R) hou_r_ (picture a clock)

S) Eskimo

T) tea (bag)

U) U-boat (submarine)

V) V neck

W) water

X) X ray (machine)

Y) question mark (?)

Z) zebra

This technique is used so that you are able to picture and remember any letter-number combination. For example, the number 312AH can be translated into maiden (using your sound technique for numbers), apple, H-bomb. An Info-Chain for this number-letter combination would be: Seeing a young maiden made out of apples, then seeing an H-bomb blast and apples coming from the blast (funny?). Here is another example:

Z105P21

Using the Alphabet Pictures, Z = zebra, P = pea

Info-Chain Association   See a zebra with a tassel (105) on; then see a tassel with peas all over it; finally, see a net (21) filled with a ton of peas.

TAKING CARE OF BUSINESS

APPOINTMENTS

The busy executive is expected to know his schedule as well as his or her secretary knows it. This task can be conquered with a simple memory technique. The basic way that you handle appointments is to set up cues that represent the week. Most memory books have elaborate systems that would take the reader at least several months to master just the basics. The technique you are about to learn uses Info-Chains to guide you through the day.

The executive needs a technique to remind him about only the appointment. The other information is usually automatically remembered.

The technique uses the same type of method to picture days of the week. Once the days of the week are pictures in your mind, it is easy to Info-Chain events during the day. Consider the following:

M T W Th F S Su

Using your Alphabet Pictures, and for some letters, your imagination, you can have a point to connect your Info-Chains to the days of the week. The pictures are:

M = ember;   F = fish,

T = tea;   Sat = sat (on a chair);

W = water;   Sun = sun

Th = Thor;

What you want to do is to create an Info-Chain for each day of the week. For example, if you were to see Mr. Joan for the first appointment on Monday, you would connect Monday and Mr. Joan. Using the method, Monday would be represented by an ember and Mr. Joan could be pictured as a loan book (you can picture a loan-payment book). The Info-Chain association would be: You would feed the embers of a fire by throwing a loan book into it.

If you have to go to the bank on Monday, you can continue to Info-Chain bank to loan book.

You could see the people in the bank exchanging loan books instead of money. With this method you could build up your Info-Chain of things to do for that day.

Remember that associating other information will really not be necessary because you need only a reminder for the appointment, etc.

Consider the following schedule:

M	T	W
Mr. Keith	Business College class	day off
meeting	bank	
Ms. Ruddy	meet boss at airport	

Th	F	Sat
Mr. Goldberg	No appointments	mow lawn
Mr. Weiner		shop for present

Sun
town meeting

Using the pictures representing the days of the week, the setups for the Info-Chains are:

1) For Monday, see yourself using embers (M, Monday) instead of a key (Keith) in your door; see many keys instead of people in a meeting; imagine a meeting in muddy waters (for Ruddy).

2) For Tuesday, imagine tea bags (for Tuesday) walking into a school for class; then see a class being held in a bank safe (for bank); see a safe meeting the boss at the airport.

3) For Wednesday, don't use anything. It's your day off! Funny you don't need a memory technique for this one.

4) For Thursday, see Thor breaking up a gold iceberg; see a giant iceberg eating a wiener (frankfurter).

5) For Friday, see a fish at regular work (maybe at a desk working).

6) For Saturday, picture a mower sitting on a chair (SAT), see a mower, by itself, mowing the lawn (wishful thinking); then see that mower buying a present in a store.

7) For Sunday, see the sun in a town meeting (a hot meeting?).

If you really are worried about the time, you can include it in your Info-Chain. For example, you are to meet Mr. Wolf at 9:05 A.M. on Tuesday. The Info-Chain is the following: See a tea bag instead of a wolf in the forest; using your sound system for numbers in the Info-Chain, then see the wolf playing with a puzzle (9:05 = *puzzle*) for the time. It is that simple!

If you have to include A.M. or P.M., just picture A.M. as a breakfast or P.M. as a dinner in your Info-Chain.

Enjoy and use the Appointment Technique in your business life. Start NOW!

THE RAM METHOD FOR YOUR BRAIN

The term RAM, in the computer industry, means Random Access Memory. This means the computer can randomly choose data from any memory bank, without going through each of the segments of the computer's memory from the first segment to the last. You are now going to learn a technique for your memory that works the same way. I call it Info-Spacing. In English that means you are going to develop individual spaces for retrieving information.

The memory trainers in history called this method variously the cue, the hook, the peg, or the hieroglyphic idea. Memory trainers use this method to remember information ranging from speeches to events in history.

You start with our famous sound system and build on that method. You will build pictures to associate information and be able to recall this information very quickly.

Remember, this method is a temporary one because the purpose of this and any other memory device is to get the information into your Long-term Memory.

To build our first Info-Spaces you look at the sound system. The first Info-Space has the sound T or D. You are looking for a picture that you will always use for the number 1 space. Our Info-Space for number 1 is Tea. The reason you use the word "Tea" is that you need a picture that is paired to the number 1. Tea can only translate into the number 1 because the only sound for number 1 is T or D.

Once you have that picture you can associate information to that image. If you look at Tea, you could picture a tea bag or anything that represents Tea in your Mind's Eye.

You are using your sound system as building blocks to create the Info-Spaces. If learned correctly, the sounds will actually fade away and you will know the Info-Spaces without thinking about the sounds in the first place.

Let us look at the second Info-Space. Our building block for 2 is the sound N. You will look for a word that can translate only to the number 2, like Noah. This can be pictured as the ark or anything associated with Noah.

Next is Info-Space number 3, which can be pictured as the month of May. The reason is the sound that represents 3 is the letter M. Following the methods outlined for the first three Info-Spaces, let me give seven more to complete your first ten Info-Spaces.

1 = Tea	4 = Hare
2 = Noah	5 = Wall
3 = May	6 = Shoe

7 = Key	9 = Pa
8 = Wave	10 = Dice

Once you go over the first ten Info-Spaces and realize why they complete the requirements of the building of the spaces, you will have a better mental set for learning the Info-Spaces. The Info-Spaces will eventually become pictures in your mind. When this happens it will be easier to use them in your business life. To get to this point you need to know the sound system and use the 1-2-5 Review Technique so that the Info-Spaces become part of your Long-term Memory.

To repeat, with the 1-2-5 Review Technique you review the material only once on the first day, the second day, and finally the fifth day. Once you learn Info-Spaces you then can use them over and over again to help you remember information paired with a sequential number. When you know this technique you will have a very helpful business skill at your command.

Finally, it is important to use the pictures and numbers for the Info-Spaces I give you because the pictures have been used for many years with success.

Here is an interesting business example: If your company has ten branches in different cities around the world, the company probably refers to them by number one, two, etc. It would be nice to be able to learn the cities by number. Let us look at the following branch numbers:

# 1) New York	# 6) Atlantic City
# 2) Chicago	# 7) Cairo
# 3) Paris	# 8) Miami
# 4) London	# 9) San Francisco
# 5) Atlanta	# 10) Washington, D.C.

You can learn these branches of your company quickly with Info-Spaces. It does not make a difference whether you start with number 1 or number 8. As long as you know the Info-

Spaces, information can be given in any order. This is not just a parlor trick but a tool for your career advantage.

First, you take the first branch, New York, which is the #1 spot. You can represent New York by using Replacement. You could picture the Empire State Building or anything that would remind you of New York. Now the Info-Space for number 1 is a Tea, so you just associate the two. You see, by using the Empire State Building as a **Tea** bag you would have a good association.

Remember to see the association, and then just go on to the next one. The next branch you would want to learn is #8, which is Miami. Well, you know that the picture for #8 is **Wave** and now associate it with Miami. You could see a giant **Wave** engulfing Florida and Miami. This would be enough to complete the association.

Let us associate the rest of the cities. For a real challenge, let's do it out of order:

#3-May to Paris—See the Eiffel Tower attached to your May calendar.

#9-Pa to San Francisco—See your father as the Golden Gate Bridge.

#7-Key to Cairo—See a giant key instead of the Pyramids.

#2-Noah to Chicago—See Noah's Ark in Chicago.

#10-Dice to Washington, D.C.—See two dice instead of the White House.

#5-Wall to Atlanta—See a giant wall along the Alantic Ocean (for Atlanta).

#4-Hare to London—Instead of Big Ben, see a rabbit.

#6-Shoe to Atlantic City—See yourself throwing a pair of shoes instead of dice in Atlantic City.

If you have followed my associations, you will feel very confident and assured that you know the cities paired with the numbers. Just think, what is the city paired with #5 or #7? If you had trouble, just go back and associate again.

Are there more Info-Spaces after the number 10 that you can use for different business purposes? The answer is yes! I will give you the following to complete your list of fifty Info-Spaces. Remember, use the pictures I give you because they are time-tested and they work! Here they are:

11 = Toad	31 = Maid
12 = Tin	32 = Money
13 = Dam	33 = Mummy
14 = Tar	34 = Mayor
15 = Doll	35 = Mill
16 = Tissue	36 = Match
17 = Tack	37 = Mike (microphone)
18 = Thief	38 = Movie
19 = Tub	39 = Map
20 = News	40 = Rice
21 = Hand	41 = Rat
22 = Onion	42 = Rain
23 = Enemy	43 = Rum
24 = Winner	44 = Roar
25 = Nail	45 = Rail
26 = Wench	46 = Rash
27 = Ink	47 = Rug
28 = Navy	48 = Roof
29 = Nip	49 = Robe
30 = Mice	50 = Lace

To help you learn the following Info-Spaces, I will tell you what I picture for these spaces. This will help you learn them faster and the pictures I give you will work better. Here they are:

11 = Toad—a small frog

12 = Tin—a tin can

13 = Dam—a giant dam

14 = Tar—pouring tar

15 = Doll—giant doll

16 = Tissue—a big sheet

17 = Tack—tack an object

18 = Thief—a big thief

19 = Tub—a big tub

20 = News—a newspaper

21 = Hand—a hand

22 = Onion—a big onion

23 = Enemy—an enemy

24 = Winner—a winner

25 = Nail—a nail

26 = Wench—a wench

27 = Ink—ink

28 = Navy—a ship

29 = Nip—taking a nip

30 = Mice—mice

31 = Maid—a maid

32 = Money—many bills

33 = Mummy—a monster

34 = Mayor—mayor

35 = Mill—a large mill

36 = Match—a large match

37 = Mike—microphone

38 = Movie—a movie

39 = Map—a map

40 = Rice—a large bowl of rice

41 = Rat—a large rat

42 = Rain—a heavy shower

43 = Rum—a bottle of rum

44 = Roar—of a lion

45 = Rail—a railroad

46 = Rash—on your skin

47 = Rug—a rug

48 = Roof—a roof

49 = Robe—a robe

50 = Lace—a piece of lace

You can create more Info-Spaces as the need arises. Using them can be a creative experience. You will have them at hand for every business problem. You could use them to remember an agenda for the big meeting for which you have a few minutes' notice. It would be an easy task once you have learned your Info-Spaces.

When you use this technique in business, there will be a few people jealous of your ability. This is to be expected. Remember, the bottom line in memory and in business is confidence. So go to the meeting and remember the material and you will have the business advantage.

Speaking about agendas, here is how to remember one: Take the agenda and associate the elements with your Info-Spaces.

Board Meeting April 18, 1992

AGENDA
—Welcome
—Approval of March 12, 1992, minutes
—Committee reports
—New business

The first part of the agenda is the date. April is the fourth month, so 4-18 can translate to ratify (using the number technique). Associate ratify to **Tea** (representing number 1). You can see yourself ratifying a tea bag in an office. If you have to remember the year, just add the digits and translate the number into a new picture (maybe 4-18-92 ratify-bun). When you are recalling the number, Natural Memory will tell you the digits for the year.

The next part of the agenda is the welcome. Associate welcome with the Info-Space for number 2. See **Noah** welcoming the people in the meeting. Approval is the next part of the agenda, so associate approval to **May.** Maybe see yourself approving with a stamp, a calendar with the month of May on it. The next part is reports. Associate this to **Hare.** You can see a hare carrying many reports. Finally, associate new business to **Wall.** See thousands of new business papers glued on a wall. If you review your Info-Spaces, you would find that you now know the agenda.

With Info-Spacing and a little imagination, a business person can be ready for any meeting.

Summary

A) The Sound System

1—T, D	6—J (Ch, Sh, soft G)
2—N	7—K (hard G, C)
3—M	8—F, V
4—R	9—P, B
5—L	0—Z, S (soft C)

B) To remember a number:

101150

Using the sounds, make the number into a picture. Two pictures are created from this number. They are *Toast—Towels.*

C) Associate the two pictures; maybe see someone eating many towels instead of toast.

D) Review the association.

E) Application is up to the imagination of the user.

Info-Spaces

Info-Spaces are spaces paired to numbers in order to associate information. They are created by the same sounds in remembering numbers. For example:

The sound for 1 is T or D .... #1 Tea

The sound for 2 is N .... #2 Noah

The sound for 3 is M .... #3 May

The use of this system is up to the imagination of the person who is using it. Let us take a simple example: Try to remember the first three corporate presidents of the fictitious company Jon Keith Inc. They are:

#1 Mr. Keith

#2 Mr. English

#3 Ms. Samuels

To remember the presidents in order or out of the sequence, you associate the Info-Space with the president (using Replacement).

Info-Space to President

Tea   associate   Keith (key); see yourself using a key instead of a tea bag.

Noah   associate   English (Big Ben); see Big Ben walking into Noah's Ark.

May   associate   Samuels (some mules); see May calendars in a field instead of some mules. If you have to remember Ms., you can see some mules trying to eat the grass but missing (Ms.).

When you have the presidents connected with the Info-Spaces, they will soon become part of Long-term Memory (with the 1-2-5 Review Technique). You will find that you will be able to recall the position and the president with ease.

Reading Comprehension

This is one of the major problem areas in business. In this section I will show you the best memory technique for remembering reading material. I have streamlined the classic memory technique to a method that will save you 50 percent of your energy. This stems from my research in this field and my ability to perform memory demonstrations. I don't expect you to run out and demonstrate remembering a magazine in one hour, but I do expect you to apply the technique for remembering reading material in your business life.

I found an unusual way to begin to train one's memory for remembering reading material. I call it the Magazine Exercise.

THE MAGAZINE EXERCISE

Let's start by defining the terms you are going to use:

Element—Any major point of an article or picture that immediately makes an impression on the mind.

Unit—Two elements linked together.

To start the exercise you should pick a news magazine that has many photos in it. What you are going to do is similar to a runner stretching before a track meet. Remember, this is for the beginner who is learning the techniques for remembering reading material. You are not going to do this exercise every time you read.

Look at the magazine and select a couple of pages. You are about to select elements from the pictures on the pages. An element is any major point that makes an immediate impression on your mind. This also applies to pictures.

In this exercise you should be looking for elements in the pictures from advertisements, articles, or photo essays. I know what you are saying—"What does that have to do with reading?" The process of selecting the elements is the same for pictures as it is for printed material. The process involves actively looking for simple elements on a conscious level. The mind will pick up things subconsciously without you being aware of the process. This will add to your total memory for reading material.

Borrowing the Feature Scanning principle from the Names and Faces section of this book, you will look at the page of the magazine, drawing a giant Z with your eyes. This will force you to look at the whole page and concentrate.

Suppose our magazine page has an advertisement for a sexy car in the upper left-hand corner. On the right-hand side there is an advertisement for a computer. You look at the entire page first and choose your elements. Maybe it would be the hubcaps of the car that stand out. If so, use that element. Pick out another element. You see that the computer terminal stands out, therefore you pick that element. Now you are ready to form an association between two elements. You take the hubcaps and associate them with the computer terminal (see the terminal as hubcaps).

What you want to do now is to associate as many picture elements (elements in the pictures only) in the magazine as you can into units of two. Then associate the last element on that page to the page number. You are to use your Info-Spaces to represent the pages in the magazine. Remember, you must use the images I gave you for the Info-Spaces. They will make it easy to associate the last element on your page.

Try two pages at first, then proceed to five. You will be amazed that after the first time associating the elements of the pictures on the page, you will have an incredible sense of the entire page.

Someone could call out the Info-Space that represents a page in that magazine and you will remember basically what is on that page. In essence you have memorized that page! If you knew twenty Info-Spaces you could memorize twenty pages of a magazine. When you apply this technique to reading material you will be amazed at the results.

I would suggest you do the exercise at least three times before reading on and learning the next section. Remember, this exercise will help your mind prepare itself for the element concept.

REMEMBERING READING MATERIAL

If you read a paragraph, you will see that there are many elements (major points) in any paragraph. These points are what you will select as elements—just as you did with the elements from the pictures in the magazine. What you want to do is be able to pick the elements and associate them together in units of two. This is an exciting system because for years memory experts have been teaching people to link *all* the elements in a chain. That is too much work for a beginner (and for anyone!). By accident, several years ago, I used the idea of associating only two elements at a time (I had several units, representing the reading material in my mind, with two elements associated in each unit). To my surprise I remembered the material just as well as if I had used the classic method. With my method of associating only two elements (a unit) at a time, you do less work and the method is about 50 percent easier to learn and execute. Remember, only two elements at a time and don't rush the process.

In every paragraph there are many elements (remember, elements are the main ideas that make an impression). What I would like you to do is to read the following paragraph and pick the elements:

> Entrepreneurs are a rare breed. They start companies that produce things like a better mousetrap to the latest communications equipment.
>
> The problem is to find someone to believe in you and to give you that all important financial backing. There are support groups to help the entrepreneur get started or find backers.

The first step is to **read** the paragraph and to look for the elements that stand out in your mind. Consider the following elements:

1) entrepreneurs

2) rare breed

3) companies

4) mousetrap, communications equipment

5) financial backing

6) support groups

These are my suggestions for elements (for #4, mouse trap, communications equipment is really the same thought). Now you have to associate the elements. Here are my associations:

1) **entrepreneurs** and **rare breed**
You could see entrepreneurs as a rare bird (rare breed).

2) **companies** and **mousetrap, communications equipment**

See a giant company or companies trapped in a mouse-trap

3) **financial backing** and **support groups**

Think of a support group throwing a million dollars at you (if you find a group like that, please contact me!).

As you see, by associating elements in groups of two, you have reduced the remembering of the paragraph to three units.

If you went through the associations, you will now be able to remember most of the paragraph without hesitation. If you use the 1-2-5 Review Technique, you would have the paragraph stored in your Long-term Memory.

You will have to get used to the technique. The best way is to start slowly and then work up to a point where you can pick elements and associate in one step. You need more practice, so consider the following letter from the president of a fictitious company:

To Our Friends, Employees, and Shareholders:

This year will be the best in our company's five-year history. With our introduction of the T-25 air-conditioner line, the company can look forward to a profitable year. This air-conditioner line is a revolution in air comfort. The T-25 adjusts to the climate by providing the necessary BTU's on demand, by way of an advance computer control. This computer is manufactured in our computer plant in Tokyo, Japan, and is being produced in record numbers. Thus, our cost will be minimal, on the order of $50 per unit. With this cost factor, the T-25 will provide a projected increase in our shares on the order of 25 cents per share.

Our next project, the T-30, will, in the next five years, make this company's markets grow in France, England, and China. The T-30 is a secret project that will make our company number one in the world market.

Using the techniques, you pick the elements that you feel are important. Let us take a look at the letter. I will distinguish the elements and will share my associations. First the elements:

To Our Friends, Employees, and Shareholders:

This year will be the *best* in our company's five-year history. With our introduction of the *T-25 air-conditioner* line, the company can look forward to a *profitable year.* This air-conditioner line is a *revolution* in air comfort. The *T-25 adjusts* to the climate by providing the necessary *BTU's on demand,* by way of an advance *computer control.* This *computer* is manufactured in our computer *plant* in *Tokyo, Japan,* and is being produced in *record numbers.* Thus, our *cost* will be minimum, on the order of *$50 per unit.* With this cost factor, the T-25 will provide a *projected increase* in our shares on the order of *25 cents* per share.

Our next project, the *T-30,* will, in the next five years, make this *company's markets* grow in *France, England, and China.* The T-30 is a secret project that will make our *company number one* in the world market.

Let us list the possible elements:

1) best

2) T-25 air conditioner

3) profitable year

4) revolution

5) T-25 adjusts

6) BTU's on demand

7) computer control

8) computer

9) plant

10) Tokyo, Japan

11) record numbers

12) cost

13) $50 per unit

14) projected increase

15) 25 cents

You are now ready to associate the elements two at a time. Remember, students of mnemonics would apply the technique as they read. Take your time and you will master this technique. Here are my elements and the associations:

Elements and Associations

best—T-25   See the air conditioner wearing a first-prize medal (the best).

profitable year—revolution   See money as soldiers in a revolution.

T-25 adjusts—BTU's on demand   Make the air conditioner adjust itself as cold air blows out of its vents.

computer control—computer   See a big computer with giant hands controlling itself.

plant—Tokyo, Japan   See a plant as part of the Tokyo, Japan, skyline.

record numbers—cost   See a pile of giant records costing a lot of money.

$50—computer   Here you use the number technique, 50 = lace; maybe see a big piece of lace over a computer.

projected increase—25 cents   See a big nail (25) being projected.

These are my suggestions on how to connect the elements that I would use to start the process of remembering the letter.

If you encounter numbers in your reading, use the technique outlined in this book to picture the number. Once this is done the picture of the number can be incorporated into one of your images.

Remember, the ridiculous connections will fade away and you will remember the material perfectly.

Reading Comprehension Exercise

Read the following fictitious speech about a company's takeover, and use the technique for remembering reading material.

We are gathered together tonight to announce the corporate takeover of the R Company. The motivation of this takeover is to brighten our financial future through installation of the R Company's technological advancement in chip innovation. Our company, being the largest copier company in the world, must think of the future as our best friend when we are on the cutting edge. The R Company's RD electronic chip is a revolution in microprocessing development. With the RD chip in our copiers, our copiers will have an advantage in the marketplace. Some of the features our customers can look forward to are: perfect copiers in all ranges, once-a-year maintenance, and voice-operated controls. All in a package that will beat our competitor's prices. The takeover will cost our company $2 billion. This price will be made up in five years, according to our forecasts. With this new technology, the sky is the limit.

ELEMENTS

We are gathered together tonight to announce the *corporate takeover* of the *R Company.* The motivation of this takeover is to brighten our *financial future* through installation of the R Company's technological advancement in *chip innovation.* Our company, being the *largest copier company* in the world, must think of the future as our best friend when we are on the cutting edge. The R Company's *RD electronic chip* is a revolution in *microprocessing development.* With the *RD chip in our copiers,* our copiers will have an *advantage* in the marketplace. Some of the features our customers can look forward to are: *perfect copiers* in all ranges, *once-a-year maintenance,* and *voice-operated controls.* All in a package that will *beat our competitor's prices.* The take-over will cost our company *$2 billion.* This price will be *made up in five years,* according to our forecasts. With this new technology, *the sky is the limit.*

Associations

corporate takeover—R Company You could picture a giant company (a building) eating the R Company.

financial future—chip innovation See a giant, unusual electronic chip with a lot of money in its circuits.

largest copier company—RD electronic chip Actually see a giant copier walking with a chocolate-chip cookie (with RD stamped on it) in its mouth.

microprocessing development—RD chip in our copiers See a giant copier with a chocolate-chip cookie in its mouth developing a microchip in a dark room.

advantage—perfect copiers See the perfect copiers running in a race and having an advantage.

once-a-year maintenance—voice-operated controls You are telling the copier (using your voice) that it will be fixed in a year.

beat our competitor's prices—$2 billion See $2 billion actually beating up the competitor.

made up in five years—the sky is the limit Think of yourself as growing wings and flying in five years; the sky is the limit.

SUMMARY

Read the following passage:

In 1973 the Arab nations cut back oil production worldwide. In the U.S. the money supply was affected.

To remember the passage you first must pick out two elements. For example, two elements could be oil and money.

You see, choosing elements is really up to the individual. Taking the first two elements, you associate OIL and MONEY. Using Replacement (the art of picturing any abstract), you could see money shooting out of an oil rig or pumping dollars into your car, etc. What this will do is to set up a series of associations that will make you remember the material.

After you associate your first two elements, you proceed to the next two elements and associate them. It is important to remember to associate only two elements at a time (a unit) and that the ridiculous association will fade and you will remember the reading material.

Here is the basic technique in summary:

A) Pick elements.

B) Use Replacement to picture elements.

C) Associate ONLY two elements at a time (forming a unit).

SPEECHES

Speeches are part of business life. With Info-Spaces and Replacement you can present your speech with ease. When you make your speech and remember it without any trouble, your delivery will be more powerful. In the business world making a good presentation can improve your standing in your company. The other benefit is that you will feel more confident. When you feel this way the sky is the limit!

For example, you are making a speech about the history of memory training as a preview to a memory course for your company. First, you write the speech. When it is in a perfect form you then choose elements from the text. As a review, it is the same process you use to remember reading material. The difference is that you will connect the elements with your Info-Spaces. If you know your Info-Spaces and know how to count, you will have the confidence to deliver the speech without worry.

Your first three elements of your memory speech about the history of memory training are:

A) The Romans and how they used memory training for speeches.

B) The Middle Ages and the scholars who used memory devices.

C) The memory performers throughout history that saved the art.

You take the elements and then you associate them to the Info-Spaces. For example:

1) Your first Info-Space is Tea; imagine a giant tea bag in a Roman uniform (to represent Roman).

2) Your second Info-Space is Noah; see Noah gathering up scholars in knights' uniforms (representing the Middle Ages) two by two.

3) Your third Info-Space is May; see a big calendar (representing the month of May) as a memory performer (memory performers are just like any other performer).

As you know, a speech is sequential and so are the Info-Spaces. To remember the speech think of the Info-Spaces (1, 2, 3, etc.). This will remind you of the elements and ultimately the speech.

REMEMBERING LECTURES, CLASSES, AND SEMINARS

So far you have used a process to remember reading material, that is, picking elements and connecting them by association, and making a speech. The process of remembering a class, lecture, or seminar is the same as remembering reading material but in reverse. When you are listening to the speaker you are to take the verbal elements that impress you and connect them in the same manner as remembering reading material (two at a time). You are using your ears instead of your eyes. You don't have to give up paper and pencil, but this method will help your note-taking skill. It will take a bit of listening practice to master this skill, but it is very effective. When you are in this situation you:

A) Listen for elements.

B) Associate elements two at a time.

C) Enjoy the feeling of remembering a class or lecture.

BUSINESS ABSENTMINDEDNESS—THE ONE-SECOND TECHNIQUE

Absentmindedness is a part of business life, but you can put a dent into it. The next time you put down your keys to the storeroom or to the boss's executive room, I want you to look at the keys an extra second and see where they are. This sounds silly but this action forces you to focus your mind on the keys. You will be amazed at the improvement in remembering small details with this simple technique. The exciting part of this is that in studies of visual memory people could remember large amounts of material when using their visual Natural Memory (without memory systems). You must realize you can never eliminate absentmindedness completely but can reduce it considerably. The technique can be summarized as follows: **Take that extra second.**

Here are some examples of how to use the technique:

Where are my glasses? (Look at the glasses for one extra second.)

Did I lock the office door? (Look at that lock.)

Did I mail the boss's letter? (Next time, look at each of the letters one extra second and you will know in the future that you mailed them.)

Where did I park the car? (Take that second to look at the surroundings.)

Did I turn the computer system off? (Look at the switch for a second.)

Did I check the mail bin for the boss? (Look at the mail bin for a second.)

Did I feed the dog? (Look at the dog eating for that extra second.)

Did I take my pill? (Look at the pill container for that second.)

Did I leave the lights on in the car? (As you walk away from the car look back for that extra second.)

Remember, use this technique every day! You **can** decrease the problem of absentmindedness.

FINAL WORD

You have discovered the world of mnemonics for business. Please apply the methods you have learned in this book. Don't be afraid to use your imagination and find other ways to use the memory techniques.

See you in the office with a great memory. And keep remembering!

BIBLIOGRAPHY

Anderson, Richard C., and Gerald W. Faust. *Educational Psychology, The Science of Instruction and Learning.* New York, Toronto: Dodd, Mead & Company, 1974.

Furst, Bruno. *Stop Forgetting.* Garden City, New York: Doubleday & Company, Inc., 1972.

Keith, Jon. *Manuscripts of Memory #1.* New York: Jon Keith, 1976.

———. *Manuscripts of Memory #2.* New York: Jon Keith, 1976.

———. *Manuscripts of Memory #3.* New York: Jon Keith, 1976.

Lorayne, Harry. *How to Develop a Super-Power Memory.* New York: Frederick Fell, Inc., 1957.

Middleton, A. E. *Memory Systems New and Old.* New York: G. S. Fellows and Co., 1888.

Roth, David. *The Roth Memory Course.* New York: Independent Corp., 1918.

Yates, Frances A. *The Art of Memory.* Chicago: The University of Chicago Press, 1966.

ABOUT THE AUTHOR

Mr. Keith started his memory career as a child demonstrating memory stunts. Researching the subject, he found that a family member performed memory stunts in the 1930s. At the age of eighteen he started teaching the skill of memory privately. Today, Mr. Jon Keith is known as the man that can remember an entire magazine in one hour and teaches corporate executives.

To contact Mr. Keith write to:
Jon Keith
P.O. Box 58
Grand Central Station
New York, New York 10163-0058